AN IDEAS INTO ACTION GUIDEBOOK

Tracking Your Development

IDEAS INTO ACTION GUIDEBOOKS

Aimed at managers and executives who are concerned with their own and others' development, each guidebook in this series gives specific advice on how to complete a developmental task or solve a leadership problem.

LEAD CONTRIBUTORS	Kelly M. Hannum
	Emily Hoole
CONTRIBUTORS	Vanessa Benozzi, Craig Chappelow, Bill Gentry, Jennifer Martineau, Cynthia D. McCauley, Tracy Patterson, Ellen Van Velsor, Rola Ruohong Wei
DIRECTOR OF PUBLICATIONS	Martin Wilcox
EDITOR	Peter Scisco
ASSOCIATE EDITOR	Karen Lewis
DESIGN AND LAYOUT	Joanne Ferguson
CONTRIBUTING ARTISTS	Laura J. Gibson
	Chris Wilson, 29 & Company

Copyright ©2009 Center for Creative Leadership.

All Rights Reserved. No part of this publication may be reproduced, stored in a retrieval system, or transmitted, in any form or by any means, electronic, mechanical, photocopying, recording, or otherwise, without the prior written permission of the publisher. Printed in the United States of America.

CCL No. 444
ISBN No. 978-1-60491-064-3

CENTER FOR CREATIVE LEADERSHIP
POST OFFICE BOX 26300
GREENSBORO, NORTH CAROLINA 27438-6300
336-288-7210
WWW.CCL.ORG / PUBLICATIONS

AN IDEAS INTO ACTION GUIDEBOOK

Tracking Your Development

Kelly M. Hannum and Emily Hoole

Center for
Creative
Leadership

www.ccl.org

THE IDEAS INTO ACTION GUIDEBOOK SERIES

This series of guidebooks draws on the practical knowledge that the Center for Creative Leadership (CCL®) has generated, since its inception in 1970, through its research and educational activity conducted in partnership with hundreds of thousands of managers and executives. Much of this knowledge is shared—in a way that is distinct from the typical university department, professional association, or consultancy. CCL is not simply a collection of individual experts, although the individual credentials of its staff are impressive; rather it is a community, with its members holding certain principles in common and working together to understand and generate practical responses to today's leadership and organizational challenges.

The purpose of the series is to provide managers with specific advice on how to complete a developmental task or solve a leadership challenge. In doing that, the series carries out CCL's mission to advance the understanding, practice, and development of leadership for the benefit of society worldwide. We think you will find the Ideas Into Action Guidebooks an important addition to your leadership toolkit.

Table of Contents

EXECUTIVE BRIEF

This book provides you with the means to set development goals and to track your progress on achieving them. It can help you efficiently gather and make sense of information about your progress and avoid common pitfalls that can block your development. Tracking your development can be captured in a few steps: articulating your goal, creating an action plan, gathering information about your behavior, identifying barriers and support, and revising your action plan. Taking these steps will greatly increase the likelihood of achieving your goals.

Keeping Track Is Important

Learning and self-development are lifelong pursuits. The goals we set for ourselves shift over time. In some cases our goals change because we have achieved the results we aimed for, and in other cases they change because they are no longer relevant (perhaps because of a job or role change). Your ability to track your progress on development goals provides you with information about when enough is enough (either because you have done all you can or need to do or because the goal is no longer beneficial). Tracking your progress can help clarify which goals are leading to the

impact you desire and which need to be reconsidered, either as new goals or perhaps with new tactics. You are probably already receiving information about your development goals through formal performance systems as well as informal mechanisms (like congratulatory e-mails from colleagues or constructive feedback). It's equally likely that the information you are getting does not provide you with a comprehensive or actionable picture of your progress on goals and that you are left wondering how to plan your next steps.

This book provides you with the means to develop a goal and to efficiently gather and make sense of information about your progress on the goal. It can also help you avoid common pitfalls that can block your development, such as assuming that feedback from one person represents (or does not represent) a broader perspective.

Establishing goals and working on them mark the early stages of a development process. But often, our personal leadership development gets lost in the rush of our day-to-day activities, and we neglect it. In order to maintain momentum and achieve goals, leaders must gather and interpret information from a variety of sources. It's easy to get off track if you don't take the time to fully consider and make sense of your goals and the information you receive about your progress toward them.

The process of tracking your development can be captured in a few steps:

1. Clearly articulate your development goal in behavioral terms.

2. Create an action plan with specific actions and dates.

3. Gather information about your behavior to inform your efforts and measure your progress.

4. Identify current barriers and sources of support.

5. Revisit and revise your action plan on a regular basis.

Articulate Your Development Goal

Gandhi said that "we must be the change we wish to see in the world." The popularity of the quotation is partly due to the practical combination of aspiration with responsibility. Similarly, goal setting involves thinking about what you want to achieve and then taking responsibility for achieving that mark, perhaps through small actions that over time can have a big impact. Working on the specific elements of your goal may seem unimportant in the short run, but the specific elements can add up to changes that matter a great deal to you and/or those around you.

A Leader's Story . . .

During a recent leadership development experience, Bob learned that his direct reports think that he does not listen to them. They say that he comes in with his mind made up and appears distracted in both one-on-one and group meetings. His actions reduce their motivation and build resentment. Bob realizes that he needs to make some changes if he wants his department to produce the results his organization is asking for. He needs to improve his relationship with the people who report to him if he wants them to be successful and achieve the desired results. Bob sets a goal of engaging in more active listening behaviors: to make eye contact when people are talking during meetings, to avoid rushing to judgment on issues and let the group discussion continue, and to ask clarifying questions.

Before focusing on the details of your goal, take a moment to envision what you want. This can be something you want for yourself, your group, your organization, your community, etc. It can be something tangible (like a 10 percent growth in sales) or something more elusive (like a more innovative working environment). The goal needs to be a "stretch." It should not be too easy; it should be difficult, yet attainable. Next, articulate your goal; write it down and keep it where you will see it often. Use specific descriptions of actions you will take to achieve it.

It's a good idea to share your goal with your direct reports, your peers, and your boss so that you can solicit their support and feedback. You'll be monitoring and noting your own behavior, and you can ask others to tell you what they observe about your actions across a range of formal and informal situations. When you feel that you've successfully changed your behavior, you can use a formal assessment (like a 360-degree feedback process) to gather anonymous feedback about how your new behavior affects the people you work with and their perceptions about your effectiveness.

What is your specific goal? Be as descriptive as possible. Goals like "becoming a better listener" aren't specific enough to be actionable and measurable. What specific behavior do you want to change, introduce, or eliminate? Ask yourself a few clarifying questions to surface those specific actions.

Who, besides yourself, will benefit from your progress on your goal? Why is this goal important to those around you? Determining the greater benefits and impact of working on your specific goal can help keep you motivated. You'll see the big picture, and you can identify sources of feedback and information that will help you track your progress.

Goal setting involves thinking about what you want to achieve and then taking responsibility for achieving that mark.

Why is the goal important to you? How does your goal connect to your vision of success? Consider whether your goal is a short-term goal intended to move you closer to a long-term goal. Understanding the connections between smaller goals and broader aspirations can help you better clarify what you need to be doing and why. Knowing the path ahead can keep you motivated.

In what situations do you need to make the change visible? Is the behavior you want to change something that you need to display with many different types of people and in many situations, or is it something that you need to work on only with a few people or in specific situations? Knowing who will be able to see the changes, when, and in what situations will help you measure whether anyone is noticing the changes you've made.

What resources (people, books, seminars, and so on) would help you reach your goal? Identify a variety of resources that will provide you with knowledge and tools to make the necessary changes to reach your goal. For instance, if your goal is related to improving communication, then search for books and seminars with practical advice on becoming a better communicator. It's also a good idea to identify development partners who can provide you with the knowledge, opportunity, and support you need to achieve or practice behavioral changes.

Create an Action Plan

An action plan is just what it sounds like. You make one to plan the actions that you must take to realize your goal. An action plan improves your ability to reach your goal by helping you think about what you need to do, determine what resources you need to draw on, and plan for the learning you need to accomplish. Your plan should incorporate ways in which you can gather the lessons that will help you develop your skills as a leader. For example, you can

- learn from a challenging situation
- learn from ongoing feedback (including assessments)
- learn from a role model, mentor, or coach
- learn from reading publications or attending courses and seminars

An action plan helps you track your development by giving you milestones against which you can measure your progress. Below are some suggestions for writing an action plan.

- Think about what you want to achieve and what you can do differently in order to get there. Ask people to give you ideas and input about the skills and knowledge you need to improve.
- Set a clear, specific, and achievable goal.
- Review your progress regularly and update your goal to match your current situation.
- Celebrate your successes and learn from your setbacks.

In addition, you can use the Action Plan Checklist or the Action Plan Worksheet (or both) to organize your thoughts.

Action Plan Checklist

These are elements to include in your action plan.

- ❏ Your goal, in measurable terms
- ❏ People who are in a position to notice changes related to your goal (your boss, direct reports, peers, clients, etc.)
- ❏ Situations in which you will make changes
- ❏ Your development partners (those with whom you will share your goal, your progress, your successes, and your barriers; those who can provide support, encouragement, challenge, and feedback)
- ❏ What you need to do (or not do) in order to achieve your goal (What should you start, stop, or continue doing?)
- ❏ Resources that are available to help you
- ❏ Barriers you anticipate encountering in your development efforts and your plans to deal with those barriers
- ❏ Milestones or indicators that will let you know you are making progress
- ❏ Your plans to gather and utilize feedback

Action Plan Worksheet

Goal	
Target Audience	
Target Situations	
Development Partners	

Name the things you plan to start, stop, and continue doing in order to achieve your goal.

Start	
Stop	
Continue	

Describe the resources (internal and external) available to you, the barriers you anticipate, and your plans to overcome them.

Resources Available	
Barriers Anticipated	
Plan to Overcome Barriers	

Explain how you will measure your progress. What will success look like? How will you gather information to gauge your progress?

Milestones	
Feedback Plan	

Get the Information You Need

After you have created your action plan, you need to gather information about your behavior and its impact on others. CCL's situation-behavior-impact (SBI) model of feedback is a proven way to gather such information (see the box on page 15).

Asking for SBI-type feedback lets people know you are interested in receiving feedback and provides a safe and useful framework for them to provide it. You may also want to gather different kinds of observations, such as more general impressions about whether what you're doing is having a positive or negative effect and getting the results you want. General comments may not help you fine-tune changes, but they can let you know whether you're on the right track.

You may want to get feedback in specific situations. For example, if you are trying not to interrupt others in meetings, ask someone to count the number of times you interrupt in a meeting or to give you a sign when you interrupt in order to focus your attention on what you're doing. In order to gather feedback that you can use, you need to determine the kinds of information you need and how it would be most helpful to receive it.

Think about how you can gather information in different ways, from different perspectives, or both. It's common for different people to interpret the same situation and behavior differently. This can be especially true if you work with many different types of people and in a variety of settings. For instance, you may work across many time zones, with people from different cultural backgrounds, or with people having different educational or work experiences. There can also be different perspectives depending on how you interact—face-to-face because you work in the same building, for example, or virtually because you work on different

Feedback the SBI Way

⇒ **Situation.** Describe the situation. To get helpful feedback, ask the person from whom you want a response to capture and clarify the specific situation surrounding your action. When and where did he or she observe you? What was the subject of the conversation?

⇒ **Behavior.** Focus on the behavior. A clear picture of your behavior is crucial to good feedback, but it's often difficult for others to focus on your behavior and not assign motives. Ask people who give you feedback to use action verbs in describing your behavior, such as "you kept interrupting other people in the meeting" rather than "you were rude during the meeting."

⇒ **Impact.** Talk about the impact. Ask the person who gives you feedback to express how your actions personally affected him or her. This will help you see your actions from the perspectives of others. The impact of being interrupted might be stated thus: "When you interrupted me, I thought you didn't care what I had to say. I felt hurt and angry."

continents. When you work face-to-face with people, you provide nonverbal signals that give them additional information that other people don't get if they interact with you only by phone or e-mail. Give some thought to the different people with whom you work and how you work together, and then gather information that represents a broad range of perspectives.

As you gather feedback and comments, keep notes or a journal to record your observations about your actions and their effect on others. Comparing your perspective with that of others helps you develop self-awareness regarding your own behavior and awareness about multiple perspectives and interpretations (even if you do not share them). When you successfully develop a high level of self-awareness regarding your own behavior and combine that with an awareness of how your behavior is interpreted by others (when you can see your behavior as others see it), you can more effectively monitor and manage your behavior over time. Keeping notes or a journal provides a place for you to reflect on your actions and gives you an opportunity to better understand when and why you have difficulty changing certain behaviors. You may begin to see trends in your behavior that you can address or modify on the way to achieving your goal.

When you can see your behavior as others see it, you can more effectively monitor and manage your behavior.

To Be or Not to Be . . . Anonymous

One aspect of the information-gathering process to consider is whether or not the information needs to be anonymous. This will depend on your situation and the type of information you want to gather. For instance, if you want to know whether you have improved your ability to inspire others, people may feel more comfortable providing that information anonymously.

Your level in the organization may also be a factor. If you're a senior leader, perhaps a member of the executive team, people may be reluctant to share their constructive criticism with you. They might be worried about their relationship with you or your impressions of them (and the impact that might have on their careers). Perhaps it is because of this that research shows that as people reach higher organizational levels, their self-perceptions and the perceptions that others have of them become increasingly different. The higher your level, the less likely you are to have the same impression of yourself that others have of you, making feedback even more important.

Whatever your level in the organization, if you solicit feedback from your direct reports, they may not be comfortable being completely honest because of a fear of reprisal. They may use the opportunity to praise you in order to be seen in a more favorable light themselves. In these kinds of situations, providing individuals with an anonymous way to give you feedback may increase your chances of receiving honest feedback.

Strategies, with Pluses and Minuses

There are many ways to gather information, and each has advantages and disadvantages. The following are common strategies for gathering feedback and some of the advantages and disadvantages of each.

Informal conversations are helpful for collecting ongoing feedback. This approach includes asking for general feedback from the individuals and in the situations you have identified as relevant to your goal. The advantages of this approach are that it's easy to do, it allows you to follow up immediately with questions to clarify what you're hearing, and it can be done however and whenever it makes sense. The disadvantage is that it is not a systematic process, so you may not remember to ask questions that may lead you to a full understanding of the feedback provided. It can also be the case that people feel put on the spot and unable to provide a thoughtful response. Instead, they say something polite because they assume that's what you want to hear (or because they don't feel comfortable saying what they really think).

Formal interviews provide information from key people about specific areas. This approach involves seeking out feedback from individuals in a more structured manner and with a timeline in mind. As with informal conversations, an advantage of this approach is that it allows you to ask follow-up questions to clarify the message you're getting. A formalized structure can also ensure that you gather similar information from different people (so that you can compare the information you receive) and can prompt you to ask about a wider range of things than you might think of in an informal context. A formal approach also allows you to schedule a meeting time so that the person you're interviewing can prepare for the meeting. You can provide in advance the questions you intend to ask, allowing your development partners time to reflect on their experiences and prepare their remarks. The disadvantage, as in informal conversations, is that the interviewees may only say something polite in order to avoid seeming critical and upsetting you.

Providing individuals with an anonymous way to give you feedback may increase your chances of receiving honest feedback.

Formal assessments provide benchmarks for you. These can include self-assessments and multirater assessments like 360-degree instruments. For instance, if you're working on communication skills, you can use a self-assessment to track your progress against behaviors known to be indicators of good communication. An advantage of this approach is that it can offer you a tangible metric for measuring improvement and specific areas for further development. Data can be gathered from others anonymously, which may provide more candid responses (especially if you occupy a senior level in your organization). A disadvantage is that readily available assessments may not be a perfect fit. They may not measure the behaviors you need to measure in exactly the way that would be ideal for you. Some assessments have open-ended

---

Help Wanted: Feedback Facilitator

If you want anonymous feedback but formal assessments are not available to you or you've decided against them, another option is to ask someone to serve as a conduit for the feedback. This feedback facilitator gathers feedback and then shares it with you in a way that doesn't identify what particular individuals have said.

---

questions, but others have no way to provide you with specific examples of when you did something particularly well (or not), making the transfer of what you see in the assessment to your day-to-day context more difficult.

Where to Seek Information

Seek information from a variety of sources and in a variety of ways. Who is likely to witness or experience your behavioral changes? Does your goal target interactions with a group or an individual? If so, get information from that group or that person, as well as from people or groups that could offer an external perspective on the interactions. People you might gather information from include the following:

- Direct reports
- Peers
- Boss
- Board members
- Teams and task forces
- Mentors
- Coaches
- Others in the organization you interact with, from receptionist to CEO

- Individuals outside the organization: clients, customers, partners, collaborators, volunteers, etc.
- Others with different backgrounds: department, ethnicity, country of origin, language, gender, etc.

You can focus your feedback efforts to include specific situations or contexts that are particularly important or relevant to your goal. Consider what specific information would be helpful to seek from the various sources or people you could ask. Use the worksheet on page 21 to list individuals, groups, and other information sources to consider. Next to each, indicate what kind of information would be helpful to gather (including when and how to gather the information).

Seek information from a variety of sources and in a variety of ways.

Interpreting and Using Information

Once you have gathered your information, the following suggestions will help you interpret and use it:

Understand the context of the information. Context matters when you are gathering information. Consider, for example, when and how you interact with the person providing information. There may be something about the context that triggers you to act (or not act) in certain ways. Keeping and referring to your journal may help you see patterns related to context.

Understand "other" perspectives. Our interactions with people are based on a variety of factors, including our behavior and values and those of the other person. Many leadership development programs emphasize self-awareness, but another important

Gathering the Information

Development Goal:

People to gather information from	What information to gather (about specific instances, overall feedback, performance data, etc.)	When to gather the information	How to gather the information (informal conversation, formal interview, formal assessment)

component is other-awareness. Before deciding someone is wrong about you or just doesn't understand, try to consider the situation from his or her perspective. It is not uncommon for people with different experiences and values to perceive a situation or a behavior differently. Before dismissing a different perspective, try to understand it. You may want to ask the person directly about how your behavior has an impact on him or her. If you don't feel comfortable asking directly, you can talk to people who can offer insight into that perspective. Keep in mind that until you ask people directly, you will not know their perspectives.

Develop themes and patterns. Gather the information from different sources, and look at it all together. Are there certain themes and patterns that stand out to you? What are you doing well, and what needs improvement? Does the information provide a consistent picture of your behavior, or is there evidence that there are differences? If there are different themes and patterns depending on where or how the information was gathered, what is the source of the difference? Is it because you behave differently in different situations or with different people? Or might different groups have different perspectives on or interpretations of your behavior?

Decide what information to act on. As you review the information about your behavior, there may be multiple actions you could take. It is important to remember that while there may be things that are not ideal, they may not require action at this point in time. Consider what is important to your success and to the success of your organization. What are you able to change? What do you have the resources and support to change?

Use the worksheet on pages 24–25 to apply these suggestions to your own development goal.

Identify Barriers and Sources of Support

Change is not easy. Identifying barriers you are likely to encounter on the path to your goal can help you avoid them or be better prepared to face them when they arise. Barriers can take many forms. For instance, we have all developed habits that prevent us from achieving what we want to, but that are difficult to break. Making a change usually involves breaking a routine that is comfortable. Identifying aspects of the change you want to make that may not be comfortable or easy will enable you to develop a strategy to avoid or cope with internal obstacles. For instance, you may have identified contacting your direct reports more often as part of your goal, but you dislike making phone calls. By identifying making phone calls as something you dislike, you can plan to use a strategy other than phone calls to check in and make contact, schedule calls in a way that will minimize what you do not like, or plan to reward yourself to counter the unpleasantness.

Lack of time is often identified as an obstacle to change. If you anticipate lack of time as a barrier, plan for it. Connecting your goal to something important can help you see small activities as having a higher priority, and thus more deserving of your time. Changing from an "all or nothing" attitude to a "one day at a time"

A Leader's Story . . .

Bob leads a large and globally diverse department, with teams located in several different countries. He needs to know whether his efforts to be a more active listener are as effective with his teams in Germany and Japan as they are with his U.S. team. Bob specifically solicits feedback from key people on each team after meetings to better understand and adjust his efforts for each situation.

Interpreting the Information

Development Goal:

Context of Feedback

What was the situation in which you received the feedback? What behavior was seen as effective or ineffective by others in that context? Why?

Are there clues from the context that might help explain why your behavior was or was not effective in that instance?

Perspectives

How much do you know about the other people's perspectives? How might their perspectives differ from yours? What are ways you could better understand their perspectives? What are ways you could better articulate your perspective?

Assume that their perspectives are valid. How might you modify your behavior to reach your goal?

Themes and Patterns

What themes are emerging from the feedback regarding your attempts to change your behavior? What is improving? How do you know? What continues to be an area for development (or has become a new one)? On what are you basing that conclusion?

Are there certain contexts in which your behavior change is more successful than in others?

Do certain people react more positively or negatively to your behavior change than others? If so, can you determine why?

How do the perceptions of others align with your own perceptions of your behavior change? If there are differences, what do you know about the other perspectives?

Start, Stop, or Continue Doing

Based upon this feedback, what will you start doing, stop doing, or continue doing in order to reach your goal?

attitude can also help. That may mean spending only ten minutes a week working on your goal—but during that ten minutes, you are absolutely committed to working on your goal.

Other barriers to your progress can be external, such as limited resources or individuals or groups that are not supportive of the changes you want to make. Identifying these early on increases the likelihood that you will be able to develop a plan for circumventing or addressing these challenges.

An effective way to deal with barriers is to identify sources of support. The best support for you will depend on your preferences, your situation, and the type of goal you are pursuing. Support can take many forms, and you can employ different types of support, especially for goals that are difficult to achieve. Emotional, cognitive, and physical support are all important. For emotional support, identify people or activities that inspire you and leave you feeling energized. Cognitive support can help you get ideas for overcoming obstacles or challenging your own assumptions. It might take the form of a mentor or coach, or it may just be a matter of being sure to use the resources you've identified in your action plan. Physical support is a matter of taking care of yourself so that you'll be able to tackle challenges.

Revise Your Action Plan

Once you have gathered information about your progress, you can fine-tune your goal or set a new goal. Remember to set rewards for yourself and celebrate your successes. If you are working toward a long-term goal, make sure to check your intermediate goals against your long-term aspiration to be sure you are on the right path. When you experience a setback (and you will—we all do when

A Leader's Story . . .

Every three months, Bob holds a virtual meeting with all of his teams. He knows that the virtual format and the time zone changes are challenging for him and for others. He plans ahead for several team members to observe his behavior and to provide feedback from multiple perspectives: on-site and off-site, different cultures, and different genders. He even considers tenure with the company as an important difference in perspective; that is, people who have been with the company longer may have a different view from that of newcomers.

making changes), take time to focus once more on what you want to achieve and review your actions and progress to date in order to learn from the setback by identifying the root of the problem. You will then be in a better position to revise your plan.

Pull It All Together

Learning and self-development are lifelong pursuits. You are more likely to achieve your goals if you have a system for tracking your development. Articulate your development goal and create an action plan. Gather the information you need from multiple perspectives and make sense of it. Be clear about the barriers to and supports for the changes you want to make, and revise your action plan as necessary. Following these steps will greatly increase your likelihood of success.

Suggested Readings

Browning, H., & Van Velsor, E. (1999). *Three keys to development: Defining and meeting your leadership challenges.* Greensboro, NC: Center for Creative Leadership.

Kirkland, K., & Manoogian, S. (1998). *Ongoing feedback: How to get it, how to use it.* Greensboro, NC: Center for Creative Leadership.

Martineau, J., & Johnson, E. (2001). *Preparing for development: Making the most of formal leadership programs.* Greensboro, NC: Center for Creative Leadership.

McCauley, C. D., & Martineau, J. W. (1998). *Reaching your development goals.* Greensboro, NC: Center for Creative Leadership.

Sternbergh, B., & Weitzel, S. R. (2001). *Setting your development goals: Start with your values.* Greensboro, NC: Center for Creative Leadership.

Background

The information in this guidebook is drawn from CCL's ongoing research into how individuals set and achieve leadership goals for themselves, as well as which evaluation strategies provide accurate and useful information about leadership goals. CCL's leader development model includes assessment, challenge, and support. Strategically and systematically tracking your progress toward a goal provides assessment information about how you are doing in relation to what you want to achieve.

The advice in this book is also based on CCL's strong stance that development is a process and that ongoing feedback is an important aspect of making decisions about what you should and can do. Thinking through the types of information to gather and ways to gather that information helps you stay on track. In addition, our advice reflects the importance of tapping into different perspectives in order to prompt deeper self-reflection.

Key Point Summary

Tracking your development can be captured in a few steps: articulating your goal, creating an action plan, gathering information about your behavior, identifying barriers and support, and revising your action plan.

Articulating your development goal begins with envisioning what you want. The goal needs to be a stretch—difficult, yet attainable. Write it down and keep it where you will see it often. Use specific descriptions of actions you will take to achieve it.

Then plan the actions that you will take to realize your goal. The action plan should include your goal; the target audience and situations; your development partners; things you plan to start, stop, and continue doing; resources; barriers and your plans to deal with them; milestones; and your plans to gather and utilize feedback.

After you create your action plan, gather information about your behavior and its impact on others. CCL's situation-behavior-impact model of feedback is a proven way to gather such information. In some cases, providing individuals with an anonymous way to give you feedback may increase your chances of receiving honest feedback. You can use informal conversations, formal interviews, or formal assessments to gather information from a variety of sources. Try to understand the context of the information and other perspectives, develop themes and patterns, and decide what information to act on.

Identifying potential barriers can help you avoid them or be better prepared to face them. An effective way to deal with barriers is to identify sources of support. Emotional, cognitive, and physical support are all important.

Review your action plan on a regular basis, and revise it as needed. Fine-tune your goal or set a new one. Celebrate your successes and learn from your setbacks.

Taking these steps will greatly increase the likelihood of achieving your goal.

Ordering Information

TO GET MORE INFORMATION, TO ORDER OTHER IDEAS INTO ACTION GUIDEBOOKS, OR TO FIND OUT ABOUT BULK-ORDER DISCOUNTS, PLEASE CONTACT US BY PHONE AT 336-545-2810 OR VISIT OUR ONLINE BOOK-STORE AT WWW.CCL.ORG/GUIDEBOOKS.

The articles in LiA *give me insight into the various aspects of leadership and how they can be applied in my work setting.*

Clayton H. Osborne
Vice President, Human Resources
Bausch & Lomb

LiA *sparks ideas that help me better understand myself as a leader, both inside and outside the organization.*

Kenneth Harris
Claims Director
Scottsdale Insurance Company

Leadership in Action

*A publication of the
Center for Creative Leadership
and Jossey-Bass/Wiley*

Leadership in Action is a bimonthly publication that aims to help practicing leaders and those who train and develop practicing leaders by providing them with insights gained in the course of CCL's educational and research activities. It also aims to provide a forum for the exchange of information and ideas between practitioners and CCL staff and associates.

To order, please contact Customer Service, Jossey-Bass, 989 Market Street, San Francisco, CA 94103-1741. Telephone: 888/378-2537; fax: 415/951-8553. See the Jossey-Bass Web site, at www.josseybass.com.